# Secret Places

Poems selected by Charlotte Huck

Pictures by Lindsay Barrett George

Greenwillow Books, New York

For Barbara Friedberg,
who has found her secret place
—C. H.


For Ava, with thanks
—L. B. G.

Library of Congress Cataloging-in-Publication Data

Secret places / poems selected by Charlotte Huck ;
pictures by Lindsay Barrett George.
        p.        cm.
Summary: A collection of illustrated poems about
secret places written by such authors as Elizabeth
Coatsworth, Aileen Fisher, and David McCord.
ISBN 0-688-11669-8 (trade).
ISBN 0-688-11670-1 (lib. bdg.)
1. Solitude—Juvenile poetry.
2. Children's poetry, American.
[1. Solitude—Poetry.
2. American poetry—Collections.]
I. Huck, Charlotte S.
II. George, Lindsay Barrett, ill.
PS595.S764S43        1993
811.008′09282—dc20
92-29014        CIP        AC

Gouache paints were used for the full-color art.  The text type is Goudy Modern.

Printed in Singapore by Tien Wah Press     First Edition     10 9 8 7 6 5 4 3 2 1

# CONTENTS

# INTRODUCTION

All of us have secret places: joyful places that we love intensely, or places of refuge where we run to hide, or places visited only in our imaginations.

Some places are those we make ourselves, such as tree houses or chair houses. Others are special containers where we keep our most precious things. And still others are the ''safe-kept memories'' of special places, events, or stories.

In this book various poets describe their love for a secret place, whether it is a bed of autumn leaves or a special rock or a sand gully. Perhaps their special places will make you think of your secret place.

*Charlotte Huck*
REDLANDS, CALIFORNIA

## THE MAPLE

In our big maple tree
There's a platform Father made,
And little seats high in the boughs
Where, in the deepest shade,
Inside the great, green thimble
My friends can climb with
                    me
To sit a while and whisper
Within the whispering tree.

ELIZABETH COATSWORTH

# HIDING PLACE

Down among the cobwebs, at the roots of grass

Green and creepy quiet, dewy beads of glass

Little spiders spinning, beetles bumbling through

Ants in hurry-scurries, bustling on my shoe

Tiny flowers bending when the bees weigh them down

And bouncing up fluttering the butterflies around

Down among the cobwebs and grasshopper spittle

I can hide and peek around and be glad I am little.

NANCY DINGMAN WATSON

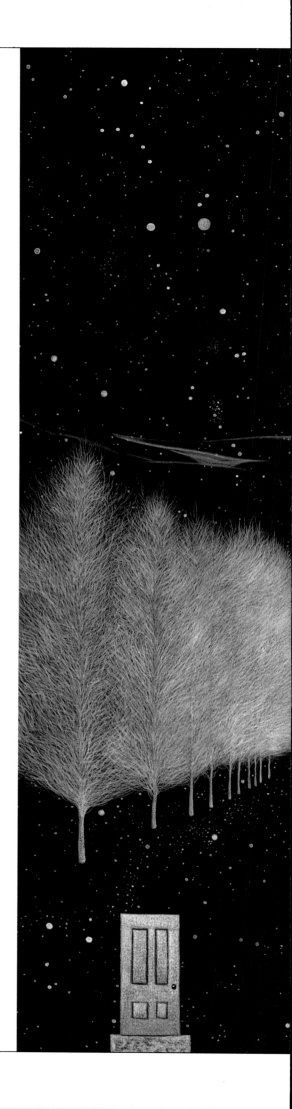

# A PATH TO THE MOON

From my front door there's a path to the moon
that nobody seems to see
tho it's marked with stones & grass & trees
there's nobody sees it but me.

You walk straight ahead for ten trees or so
turn left at the robin's song
follow the sound of the west wind down
past where the deer drink from the pond.

You take a right turn as the river bends
then where the clouds touch the earth
close your left eye & count up to ten
while twirling for all that you're worth.

And if you keep walking right straight ahead
clambering over the clouds
saying your mother's & father's names
over & over out loud

you'll come to the place where moonlight's born
the place where the moonbeams hide
and visit all of the crater sites
on the dark moon's secret side.

From my front door there's a path to the moon
that nobody seems to see
tho it's marked with stones & grass & trees
no one sees it but you & me.

bp NICHOL

## OUTDOORS

My favorite place—
the hidden den
in the shrubbery,
where I creep in
and sit with my
book
and my doll
Gwendolyn,
   and my little
   striped bag
   of jelly beans
   from Horning's.

CLAUDIA LEWIS

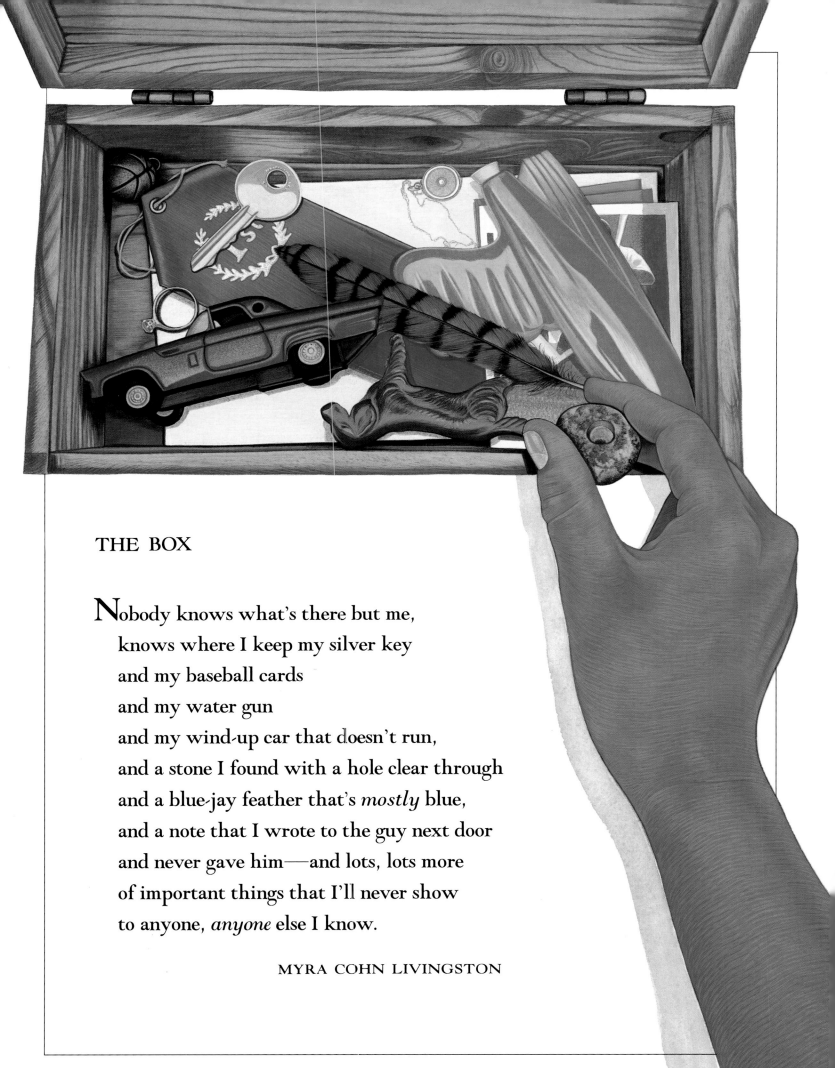

## THE BOX

Nobody knows what's there but me,
knows where I keep my silver key
and my baseball cards
and my water gun
and my wind-up car that doesn't run,
and a stone I found with a hole clear through
and a blue-jay feather that's *mostly* blue,
and a note that I wrote to the guy next door
and never gave him—and lots, lots more
of important things that I'll never show
to anyone, *anyone* else I know.

MYRA COHN LIVINGSTON

SOLITUDE

I have a house where I go
When there's too many people,
I have a house where I go
Where no one can be;
I have a house where I go,
Where nobody ever says "No";
Where no one says anything—so
There is no one but me.

A. A. MILNE

## THE ISLAND

They mowed the meadow down below
Our house the other day
But left a grassy island where
We still can go and play.

Right in the middle of the field
It rises green and high;
Bees swing on the clover there,
And butterflies blow by.

It seems a very far-off place
With oceans all around:
The only thing to see is sky,
And wind, the only sound.

DOROTHY ALDIS

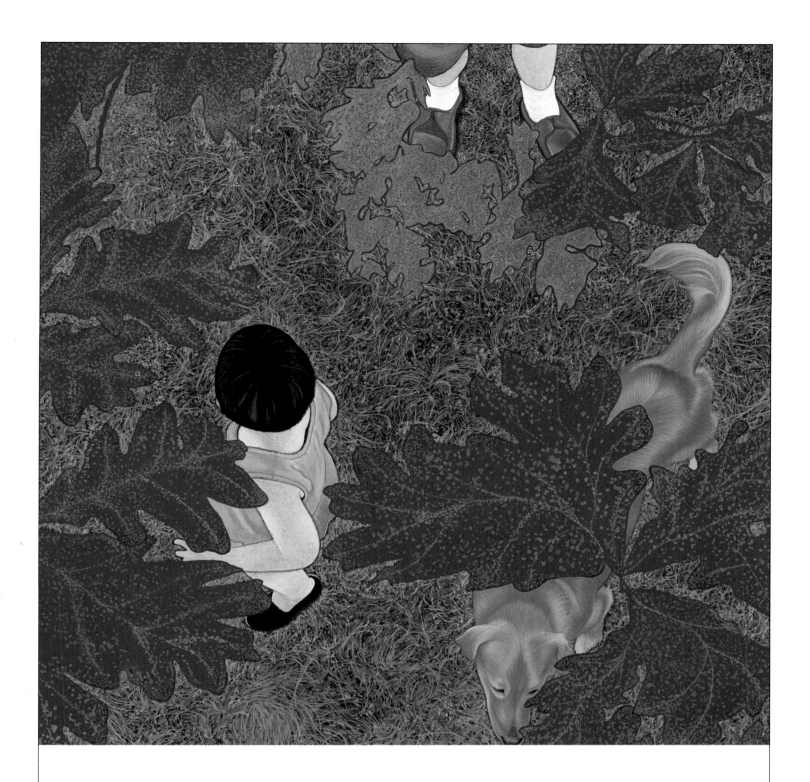

## THE HIDEOUT

They looked for me
and from my nook
inside the oak
I watched them look.

Through little slits
between the leaves
I saw their looking
legs and sleeves.

They would have looked
all over town
except—
I threw some acorns down.

AILEEN FISHER

## THE CHAIR HOUSE

When it's raining,
            And raining,
                        And raining,
With a drip and a drizzle and a drop,
The porch is so cool and so pleasant,
The rain falls, hippity hop,
And I take a porch chair and
                        upturn it,
With a blanket to serve as a door,
And I put in a pillow or pillows
To make a soft place on the floor.

There it is, dark and safe: it's an igloo,
Or perhaps it's an African hut.
I crawl in and the door drops
                        behind me,
It's a wonderful house, but…but…,
It's so small, there's no place to go to,
It's so dark, there is nothing to do,
So soon I lift up the blanket,
And, looking about me, crawl through.

Yet though I don't stay, I still love it,
I dream of my chair house at night,
And I hear the rain calling
And falling,
As I curl myself up, out of sight.

ELIZABETH COATSWORTH

## IF ONCE YOU HAVE SLEPT ON AN ISLAND

If once you have slept on an island
    You'll never be quite the same;
You may look as you looked the day before
    And go by the same old name,

You may bustle about in street and shop;
    You may sit at home and sew,
But you'll see blue water and wheeling gulls
    Wherever your feet may go.

You may chat with the neighbors of this and that
    And close to your fire keep,
But you'll hear ship whistle and lighthouse bell
    And tides beat through your sleep.

Oh, you won't know why, and you can't say how
    Such change upon you came,
But——once you have slept on an island
    You'll never be quite the same!

RACHEL FIELD

## THIS IS MY ROCK

This is my rock
And here I run
To steal the secret of the sun;

This is my rock
And here come I
Before the night has swept the sky;

This is my rock,
This is the place
I meet the evening face to face.

DAVID McCORD

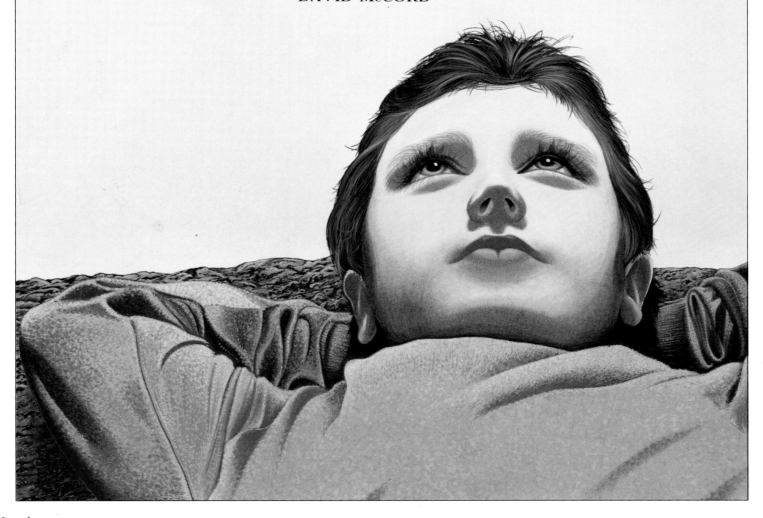

## THERE WAS A PLACE

There was a place
we'd always walk,
look at the sky,
have a long talk.

Sit on a bench,
drink a few Cokes,
listen to Dad
telling some jokes.

Now the sky's dark.
Can't see his face.
Can't hear the jokes.
There was a place.

MYRA COHN LIVINGSTON

## JEREMY'S HOUSE

Jeremy hasn't a roof on his house
For he likes to look at the stars;
When he lies in his bed
With them all overhead
He imagines that he can see Mars.

Sometimes a thunderstorm lights up the sky
And Jeremy gets soaking wet;
But he says that it's worth it
To lie in his bed
And see folks go past in a jet.

He's counting the stars in the Milky Way,
It's going to take him forever;
But Jeremy's patiently
Counting away
For he knows it's a worthwhile endeavour.

LOIS SIMMIE

## AUTUMN LEAVES

One of the nicest beds I know
isn't a bed of soft white snow,
isn't a bed of cool green grass
after the noisy mowers pass,
isn't a bed of yellow hay
making me itch for half a day—
but autumn leaves in a pile *that* high,
deep, and smelling like fall, and dry.
That's the bed where I like to lie
and watch the flutters of fall go by.

AILEEN FISHER

## SLEEPING OUTDOORS

Under the dark is a star,
Under the star is a tree,
Under the tree is a blanket,
And under the blanket is me.

MARCHETTE CHUTE

## A BOY'S PLACE

I know a place
that's oh, so green
where elephant ears
together lean;
a quiet place
that no one's seen
but me.

It's not very far
my secret spot.
I go whenever
the day's too hot
for friends or games
or a story's plot—
just me.

I leave my shoes
at home and go
over the wall
where the blackberries grow
and squoosh my toes
in the mud, with no
design.

A gentle jungle
of swamp and sky,
a curious bird
my only spy,
a place to whistle
each August by—
all mine!

ROSE BURGUNDER

## FROM *YOUR OWN BEST SECRET PLACE*

I think of
other
private
hidden
secret places
I have had.

The best one
was
a place
I used to go
when I was
little.

It was just
a sandy gully
cutting through
the hard
flat
Texas earth,
but that gully
was
a whole world
by itself
and I was
the only
person
there.

It was more like
a ditch
than a canyon
but
I'd never seen
a canyon
then
and it was
what
I thought
a canyon
ought
to be.

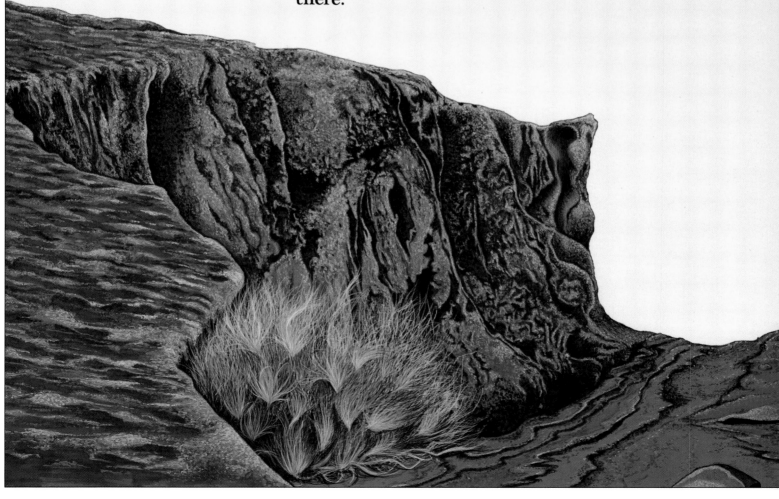

It was
deep
and wide
and the walls
were
taller
than I was,
and when
I looked up
I could only see
sky.

I always
*had* to
run
there.

I *had* to
lift
my arms up
high.

I *had* to be
barefoot
even if
sand
was burning
my feet.

Since then
I've seen
a hundred
deeper canyons
but
I still miss
that gully
that wasn't
even
a canyon
at all.

BYRD BAYLOR

## KEZIAH

I have a secret place to go.
Not anyone may know

And sometimes when the wind is rough
I cannot get there fast enough.

And sometimes when my mother
Is scolding my big brother,

My secret place, it seems to me,
Is quite the only place to be.

GWENDOLYN BROOKS

## BEING LOST

Being lost
Is the perfect way
To pass the time
On a sky blue day

When it's warm
And the open window
Uncurtains a call
Spiraling up the stairway
Hovering in the hall.
No one comes then
When they call me.
I am not there
Where they look.
I linger alone
In a place of my own
Lost
In a book.

KARLA KUSKIN

# ACKNOWLEDGMENTS

THE ISLAND by Dorothy Aldis, from *All Together* by Dorothy Aldis, copyright 1952 by Dorothy Aldis, copyright renewed © 1980 by Roy E. Porter. Reprinted by permission of G. P. Putnam's Sons.

From YOUR OWN BEST SECRET PLACE by Byrd Baylor, text copyright © 1979 by Byrd Baylor. Reprinted by permission of Charles Scribner's Sons, an imprint of Macmillan Publishing Company.

KEZIAH by Gwendolyn Brooks, from *Bronzeville Boys and Girls* by Gwendolyn Brooks, copyright © 1956 by Gwendolyn Brooks. Reprinted by permission of HarperCollins Publishers.

A BOY'S PLACE by Rose Burgunder, from *From Summer to Summer* by Rose Burgunder, copyright © 1965 by Rose Styron. Reprinted by permission of Viking Penguin, a division of Penguin Books USA, Inc.

SLEEPING OUTDOORS by Marchette Chute, from *Rhymes About Us* by Marchette Chute, published in 1974 by E. P. Dutton, copyright © 1974 by Marchette Chute. Reprinted by permission of Elizabeth Roach.

THE MAPLE and THE CHAIR HOUSE by Elizabeth Coatsworth, from *The Sparrow Bush* by Elizabeth Coatsworth, copyright © 1966 by Grosset & Dunlap, Inc. Reprinted by permission of Grosset & Dunlap, Inc.

IF ONCE YOU HAVE SLEPT ON AN ISLAND by Rachel Field, from *Taxis and Toadstools* by Rachel Field, copyright 1926 by The Century Company. Reprinted by permission of Doubleday, a division of Bantam Doubleday Dell Publishing Group, Inc., and of William Heinemann Ltd.

THE HIDEOUT and AUTUMN LEAVES by Aileen Fisher, from *In the Woods, In the Meadow, In the Sky* by Aileen Fisher, text copyright © 1965 by Aileen Fisher. Reprinted by permission of the author.

BEING LOST by Karla Kuskin, copyright © 1986 by Karla Kuskin. Reprinted by permission of the author.

OUTDOORS by Claudia Lewis, from *Long Ago in Oregon* by Claudia Lewis, copyright © 1987 by Claudia Lewis. Reprinted by permission of HarperCollins Publishers.

THE BOX by Myra Cohn Livingston, from *A Song I Sang to You* by Myra Cohn Livingston, copyright © 1984, 1969, 1967, 1965, 1959 by Myra Cohn Livingston. Reprinted by permission of Marian Reiner for the author.

THERE WAS A PLACE by Myra Cohn Livingston, from *There Was a Place and Other Poems* by Myra Cohn Livingston, copyright © 1988 by Myra Cohn Livingston. Reprinted by permission of Margaret McElderry Books, an imprint of Macmillan Publishing Company, and of Marian Reiner for the author.

THIS IS MY ROCK by David McCord, from *One at a Time* by David McCord, copyright 1929 by David McCord. First appeared in *Saturday Review* in 1929. Reprinted by permission of Little, Brown and Company and of Harrap Publishing Group Ltd.

SOLITUDE by A. A. Milne, from *Now We Are Six* by A. A. Milne, copyright 1927 by E. P. Dutton, renewed © 1955 by A. A. Milne. Reprinted by permission of Dutton Children's Books, a division of Penguin Books USA, Inc., and of Methuen Children's Books.

A PATH TO THE MOON by bp Nichol, from *Giant Moonquakes and Other Disasters* by bp Nichol, copyright © 1985. Reprinted by permission of Black Moss Press.

JEREMY'S HOUSE by Lois Simmie, from *Auntie's Knitting a Baby* by Lois Simmie, published by Western Producer Prairie Books, copyright © 1984 by Lois Simmie. Reprinted by permission of Douglas & McIntyre.

HIDING PLACE by Nancy Dingman Watson, from *Blueberries Lavender: Songs of the Farmer's Children* by Nancy Dingman Watson, copyright © 1977 by Nancy Dingman Watson. Reprinted by permission of the author.